SWEET HONEY WOMAN

HEALING IS THE NECTAR AND THE ELIXIR

Lauren Lynch-Novakovic

BookLeaf Publishing
India | USA | UK

Presentation by *BookLeaf Publishing*

Web: www.bookleafpub.com

E-mail: info@bookleafpub.com

ISBN: 9789358738636

First edition 2021

ACKNOWLEDGEMENT

First and foremost, I must acknowledge my dear sister friend, fellow poet, educator, leader, and visionary Ivory Bennett. She nudged me with the opportunity to participate in creating this book and quite literally it wouldn't exist without her! My gratitude to my parents who instilled in me a love and utilization of words. And sincere appreciation to BookLeaf Publishing for being integral in helping me publish my first poetry book- it shall not be my last!

Beyond these necessary and foundational people and components I acknowledge life itself. For providing me with experiences, challenges, and opportunities. I acknowledge God, the Universe, and my Ancestors for bestowing upon me breath and innate gifts on a life journey- and equipping me with the tools to make the most of it.

PREFACE

Sweet Honey Woman was birthed from a beautiful union of immense self-improvement and supportive friends. One night when texting my sister friend, fellow poet, and overall dynamic interdisciplinary artist, Courtney L. Black she sent me those words, "sweet honey woman." They stood out to me, spoke out to me. I immediately left the text and began writing the poem. A few minutes later I returned and sent it to her. Something about it felt so right, it completely encapsulated the journey that this book signifies. A few days later, in need of a title I had my aha moment- Sweet Honey Woman!

This book is about healing. Healing is not linear; we often hear this. But what does that really mean? Well, you will have moments of courage and others of doubt. There will be small and large victories, as well as setbacks, triggers, and things that require revisiting. There will be highs and lows, and many perceived plateaus. The result is sweet but the work to get there ain't- perfectly sums up the journey of the book!

May these poems guide you where you need direction and provide you with words to articulate your experience. May there be moments during and after reading it that ignite questions and clarity that stoke the flames of your soul.

Healing (noun)

the process of making or becoming sound or healthy again.

(adjective)

tending to heal; therapeutic.

Nectar (noun)

1. a sugary fluid secreted by plants, especially within flowers to encourage pollination by insects and other animals. It is collected by bees to make into honey.
2. (in Greek and Roman mythology) the drink of the gods.

Elixir (noun)

1. a magical or medicinal potion.
2. a particular type of medicinal solution.

We have all that we need! Define yourself and your legacy.

DEDICATION

I dedicate this book to myself, in every phase and version. My old self should be so proud, mind blown at the level of dedication to progress and growth. My future self, and every self thereafter, should look at this period and smile with warmth and glee, seeing the strength, grace, and audacity sprouting. And most importantly to my current self, fully embracing the never-ending journey and evolution. And certainly, to the reader; I hope you too can dig deep and find the dedication to and for yourself!

4.1 CRYING PRAYING ON MY FACE

An overwhelming

emotion

Not quite

sadness

It's

the

grief

The gap

Between

Knowing

And

Feeling

And

allowing space

for the lessons

to integrate

Releasing grip

For the past

to disintegrate

No one prepares you

for the grief in growth

No one outlines a picture

for the lost grey in between space

No one elaborates

for the complete detachment

No one can

for the journey is yours

No one can articulate

for the words won't encapsulate

No one can

who has not first experienced

and processed it

themselves

And for those who get it

The tenderness in silence

The warmth in holding space

The love in sending you well wishes

The power in knowing you shared a battle,

a victory

Whether together or individually

Emboldens the air

And it allows you to pick your heart up

And hold it

With thanks, reverence, and a gentleness

For it beats for you

4.3 WHEN IT HURTS SO GOOD

People learn through pain

This can be overwhelmingly toxic

Doesn't make it less true

You may experience it directly

Or witness it in someone close to you

Things will hurt

Words will sting

Action, or inaction, will cut

We will experience and endure

It is inevitable, but

We do not have to suffer

We do not have to dwell

We do not have to repeat cycles

We do not have to fail

Shifting to a place of observation

Understanding is healing

Knowing our triggers

Listening to our feelings

Pain can become a sign of transition

A challenge point to reflect and release

An opportunity to lean in and build new muscle

The signal that you are growing and to be gentle

A call to rest and pause from the hustle and bustle

It hurts so good

It means you are changing

For the better

For yourself

For a newness is upon you

Won't you welcome it in

And apply the tactics to nurse your soul back

Won't you allow it in

And listen to the wisdom in your bones

Won't you embody it within

And walk forward strengthened and emboldened

4.4 RESURRECTION

Allow the winds of change

to caress your skin

Morphing the cells

and kneading the soul within

Learn to swim in

your depth

so, you do not drown in

your emotions unchecked

Standards are not expectations

Expectations lead to disappointments

Expectations say I expect you

to move how I would move

Standards say this

This is how you will conduct yourself

to gain access and remain

Master yourself for

As within

So without

Everyone battles internally

You cannot take it personally

For you must stop and ask yourself

If they mirror me-

why did I abandon myself

4.5 UNTITLED

Release

For it is all related

And the freedom reverberated

Do the digging

Excavating

Move the mountains

What you have built,

it is faulty,

For it is not the truth

You are capable of building,

with such force and power

Now do it with the truth,

never to be devoured

Honor your strengths

Start anew

Gut it out

Cry and cleanse it

Pour in love

Every tear of salt,

makes way for sweet

Break the cycle

Create heathy patterns

Be proud of your work

Honor yourself

Have appreciation for the art,

that is also the sculptor

4.6 REMINDERS

Drink from your own well.

Taste the bitterness,

from every lesson learned.

Smell the aroma,

earthy and gritty.

Like when you finally grounded yourself-

Let it wash over you,

from the inside parts.

Like mineral deposits,

for stowed away strength,

your character and endurance built up.

Integrity and discipline.

No matter the emotion flowing in.

More silence...

There are answers there

Some LOUD

Some quiet

Some harder to swallow

Yet all true

Embrace it!

The journey is center stage

Destinations are

mere pitstops

along the way.

Enjoy every thrill

Navigate every dip

Live life to the fullest

For it is the sweetest gift!

4.7 BITTERS

You are not soiled

You were sweetened

Steeped in all your preparation

Stewed for potency

Sautéed in the secret sauce

Smoked out the impurities

The bitters

They are medicine

The hurts

The losses

The disappointments

And even the self-limitations

They were but redirection

Protection

Your spirit's rejection

of what is not yours,

not up to standard,

not vibrating with you in alignment

We want others to take it

A spoonful of sugar

makes the medicine go down

But when you take it raw

Unfiltered

Unrefined

Unaccompanied

My how brilliant

The complexity

The bitter

The sweet

The flavor

An appreciation

For the process

An understanding

Of the full embodiment

4.8 RIPENING

The reckoning

Aesthetically beautiful

Enticing

Like a plump nectarine

Hues of

      Red

            Orange

                  Yellow

But the first bite is tough

Not what expected

Or anticipated

Not to be mellow

Dramatic

But

Give it time

The yearning for

     Soft

          Sweet

               Juicy

                    Experience

You crave

You desire

Await the proper time

Is it in season yet?

We cannot rush

You can-

and will-

have what you want

When it's right

When it's ripe

When it's ready

When you are ready for it

4.9 BUTTERFLY BABY

The butterfly doesn't get tired of flying

She feels the liberation in every flap

And invites the world to witness her fragile yet bold
beauty

Her softness allows her to flutter

She gave up the heaviness of caterpillar and cocoon
long ago

Whenever she may get weary she leans into the
current and allows the air to carry her

She glides

Surrenders to the flow of the universe

And forever rides

the wave of God

She is a frequency all her own

This is why people stop in amazement and wonder

As she dances around their car sitting in afternoon traffic

While she swoops by someone on an unsuspecting walk

She shifts the tide

Captivating

Teaching us lessons

Symbolism of beauty strength and transformation

Won't you keep flying butterfly baby?

4.11 DIRECTIONS HOME

Sometimes life will knock you into a tizzy

And all of the work you've done will seem fizzy

like orange pop on a hot day,

well shaken after rolling around in the backseat of
your car.

So here I have designed a map:

10 directions home

Back to me

Back to my peace

1. Stop and turn inward, find the steadiness of your
beating heart

2. Look up and locate the sun, moon, clouds, or stars- whichever you find first, connect and trust

3. Go deep, down to the insides, at the root of why you're lost or far away. The only way out is through

4. Take as many two steps as you need to, to shake off the stagnancy and lift the vibrations

5. Follow the winding road, explore along the bend of the river, go wherever the lines are not linear, neither is your journey

6. Left of your past, leave it there

7. Right of your mind, get back to your right mind

8. Move west following the sunset on the boulevard of dreams

9. Walk up to the mirror

10. And with 3 deep breaths- inhale deeply, exhale fully- arrive. Back in your body. Home.

Home is where the heart is.

Not a physical structure, except your temple

The sacred creation and altar

Made of flesh, bone, blood, and magic

Give thanks for you were blessed with your ancestors' hands

And that's word to the poet Jasmine Mans

5.14 NINE

Divine completeness

Finality

You have finally received the lessons

Finally given yourself time and space

Finally, fully activated your power and leaned

into your faith with grace

They say indecisive, perhaps

But more often than that

You're adaptable,

      flexible,

            going with the flow

Your joy radiates and your aura glows

I hope you see what I see

And feel what I feel

One thing is for certain

You can be decided

Firmly

On you

Final form

Always forming

4.12 SOLSTICE

Happy solstice

Nourish your soul sis

Sow and plow

Pour your sadness

Into a cleansing rain

Water yourself

Let your troubled thoughts

go down the drain

with the shampoo

May your twisting

be your

organization

of thoughts.

Being alone is

vastly

different than

Feeling

L o n e l y

Solitude

It may run a number

You are best here

Harness your power

Cloaked in clarity

Women

We are the givers

And the keepers

Be sure they first exhibit effort

Chase, offering

Before you grant access

Regardless of the experience

We keep

Time

Memory

Space

All remnants

And we guard the gate

4.13 WEARY

Weary

Tattered

Torn

Stitched up

Barely hanging on

Scraps

Shreds

Remnants

Make them anew

Beautiful puzzle pieces

Of the soul

4.14 Mirror mirror

As within so without

People can only meet you

As deeply

As they've met

themselves

And what is your

frustration and disappointment

teaching you

About your own

Self-betrayal

Self-negligence

Breaking promises

Wasting time

Pretending

Drawing it out

Why do these things to yourself

By allowing someone else to

Where must you dive to see

How far must you go to comprehend?

What are you willing to give up?

Your old self for your new

Or simply lose your peace playing the fool

Mirror mirror

Do you see you

See you for who you are

Not who you were

Nor what you did

Or didn't do

See you for who you will be

Who you want to be

Who you strive towards

4.15 STORAGE

Running outta room

and time

Running out of distractions

from your mind

How long can you ignore

and avoid

and hide

and lie

Question is

how long will you keep,

barely holding to survive

Answer is

until you accept

that it is your birthright to thrive

Now

on to

unpacking

all

you store

inside

What's between who and where you are now

are merely the landmarks you'll pass,

the things you'll tell yourself, how dedicated and fast

See something like,

"I bet I can beat you home" after school with friends

Setting your sights and taking off with the wind

Like, "if I can get to this stop sign,

then make it past the fence,

I'll hop over that pothole and it's smooth sailing
from there"

Turns into, if I can open up the storage facility of my
mind,

my heart,

and my body

Just empty out the thoughts,

interrogate the stories,

and lay out all the misconceptions

Relieve myself of all the stop signs I put in place,

telling myself no-just get to that stop sign.

Uproot it's post and create a flow

of energy and momentum

Eradicate all the invisible barriers I erected,
believing I couldn't move beyond certain points and
levels-

make it past the fence.

Tear it down and reveal the freedom

and wide-open possibility

Take time to mend all the empty craters I ignored,

jumping over things yet feeling the gravity pulling
from the gaping emptiness-

hop over that pothole.

Instead taking the time to

assess, approach, and properly patch things for myself

and all others who enter my heart

to walk with sure and steady footing

Smooth sailing well that's all in perception

Life will have its ebbs and flows

It will become more manageable

dare I say magnificent

When I know I am not a storage facility that houses deception

or self-deprecation

Not a warehouse of worry

Nor a storefront of sorrow

Fully present in unshakeable joy today

Making room for brighter tomorrows

4.16 FIRST FOUR

I gazed at the letters, riddled with words.

"First four words you see here reveal your subconscious mind, go for it!"

Skimming lines

Black text

Pink and blotted color

Change

Strength

Family

Breakthrough

First, we accept and honor that the only thing constant is Change baby.

Secondary to none, the Strength of heart, endurance in playing your part.

Third time's a charm, Family is chosen, cultivated, curated, and cared for.

Four for four, Breakthroughs open every window and door. May we soar. May we never settle for the lesser and have capacity to give and receive more.

4.17 BABY GIRL

I have lived

Alive

Then alone

All of my past

Brought me to my present

On the precipice

Always said do it for the memories

Fleeting

Narrating my own story

Evolution

Everything I would change

Is on the chopping block now

Won't take it back

Because

Wisdom

Pivot

Move forward

Do better

Knowing better

Release

The guilt

The hurt

The disappointment

She did her best

And sometimes her best worst

But it was the best right

Chuckle with your heart

Smile with your soul

Allow her room for growing

And hold her during the growing pains

Oh baby girl

4.18 STRUGGLE IS NOT SYNONYMOUS WITH LOVE

For years we've been told

explicitly and subliminally

that love

must include

is righteous

only validated

when struggle is present

Lies you tell

And

I wish you well

Often we only debate this concept

in terms of romantic love yet

have we stopped to ponder?

how we've internalized the same

in our relationships with self

You are allowed to be vulnerable

In fact you must be

You are safe to shine without dimming

It is your duty

You are supported, please ask for help

You are a flower, beautiful, fragile, strong all at once

You are allowed to live in ease

In fact you must declare it

You are supposed to live in luxury

It is your right

You are capable, please apply yourself

You are a strategist, working smarter not harder and
executing the vision of your dream all at once

Yet you choose struggle

As if it's righteous

As if it is the prerequisite

As if being self-made exists

The ways in which you shut out

help

support

vulnerability

your own elevation

This is all another means to struggle

You do not have to compromise

your integrity

your vision

your basic needs and wellness

Let the light in

Let the love in

Struggle is not synonymous

4.19 HONORABLE

Your healing is honorable

Your honesty

Your transparency

You're asking the questions

Seeking the answers

Unlearning

Reprogramming

Discovering yourself buried beneath it all

Bearing your soul

Sharing your story

Rewriting the one you tell yourself

Making peace

Making a clean break

Integrating the lessons

Implementing the wisdom gained

No mistake exists

The paradigm shifts

The metamorphosis

Honorable

How you embody it

How your smile is full brightness

How you are present

Full of joy

Free flowing

You deserve it

You are a lighthouse for others

Honorable

4.20 ACROSS TIME

Dear lover,

I write this to you across time,

speaking into the future of when we will unite

May my words also reach back in time,

to the heart of you

May they reach you now,

congratulating you on your inner work

Rolling in like thunderous clouds

Filling up the space that you've opened,

for me

It is so rewarding to heal

We create sturdy foundations

We open the road for our blessings to flow

We get an opportunity to be real

Dripping in authenticity

Aroma pungent with joy

Heart beating to the steady rhythm of security

Inner child

zestful energy

of girl and boy

I write to you in the future,

perhaps I am beside you,

or in the other room

May you always smile at my words

and feel them enter you with every breath

May you be enveloped in the sweetness that seeps through my every pore

and understand that our love knows no bounds...

across time

even if

we haven't

happened

upon one another

just yet

4.21 NEW LEVEL

Bathe

Cleanse

Submerge

Baptism

Crackle of...

Orgasm

... frankincense and myrrh

Flood

Overflow

Say yes

There simply comes a time

when you are fully present

A place opens up

where you are prepared

it is within you

Here, a resounding yes

Hear how you vibrate

in harmony

with God,

Divine

Universe

whatever you may call it

whoever you may recognize

Interconnected

Intentional

Infinity

Inter dimensional

Spiritual

4.22 BULL IN A CHINA SHOP

Non stop

Senses engaged

Sight and sound

Relishing in the beauty

Aesthetically pleasing all around

A masterpiece from the heavens

Voice echoes caressing eardrums like the cascading honey that dripped, from sirens lips

Taste and touch

The sweetest flavor, complex

Absolutely insatiable

Smooth, like velvet, infused, with Shea butter

Never take your hands off

Sniffing out the bullshit

replacing it with floral notes

sweet and everlasting

Sensing

beyond the five

embodying the clairs

dedicated to the process

Reputation paints a picture

Distorted and warped

Remnants of truth

through prisms reflected off the broken glass

Slivers of mirror

Reflections

Fine China

Delicate

High value

Placed on shelf

Left for dust when in the wrong ones' possession

Not to be possessed,

just experienced and blessed

They refuse to see the possibility

Project the ambiguity

You transmute it with

Sincerity

Surety

What a soul, behold

4.23 SYNCHRONICITY

Communication of the universe

The signs of God

Waiting for you to notice,

to connect the dots

Dot the I's

Cross the T's

Lean in

for understanding becomes healing

4.24 TRIGGER

Teachable moment.

Resonate anymore?

Introspection and intentionality

Giving up the old and toxic;

Going towards the light, forward.

Emotional intelligence and evolution!

Respect the triggers, they are but tool

4.25 QUIET STORM

I hope you are caring for yourself

being introspective and loving

with you.

It sounds like it

in your voice.

I sense a calm after a storm in you-

know that you ARE

the eye of the storm.

Find your perfect peace,

and allow the things around you

to be cleared-

May your path always be ready for you

Clear to you

Clarity within you

Stand firm

Sit calm

Talk slow

Listen more

Think hard

Love gentle

Let this quiet storm stir

Inside of you

Let it remind you

And guide you

4.26 WHEN THE SMOKE CLEARS

You will crawl through a tunnel of tired.

Growth requires grieving

Heavy breathing

Chest heaving

Pain and resentment

leaving...

...imprints

and lessons.

Pathways carved out for blessings.

4.27 FULL MOON IN SCORPIO

Keep me clean

Keep me pure

Keep me steady

Keep me sure

Integrate my shadow

Loose these chains

Cut these ties

Breathe winds of change

for me to soar

Cascade and drip

Like honey

Decadent

Magnetic

Fuck it

I have the audacity

Confidence

Brilliant, you see

4.28 CAPTION

Take a moment

Recognize your breath

Inhale deeply

Exhale intentionally

Put down everything that's heavy

Allow me to say this

I am thankful you are here

I am grateful your heart beats steady

I am appreciative of your daily commitment

I speak life, love, joy, and peace over you.

Go drink some water.

Unplug.

Rest.

Recharge.

4.29 SIDEWALK

You are effectively tying yourself down to concrete

Stopping yourself from soaring to new heights

Everybody can't go

Leave them

Choose you

Move with your expansion

You'll catch them around later

Perhaps in the exact same spot

When you spin the block

Can't stop, won't stop

4.30 A CUP OF JOE

Perhaps you've snuck into my timeline

whenever I've crossed your mind?

I've smelled coffee, strongly

The most aromatic blends and grounds

Does it mean you're grounded?

5.3 SWEET HONEY WOMAN

Sweet

Honey

Woman

Sticky, sticking to you, through thick and thin, from begin to end

Pouring, giving from the very depths of her essence, spilling it all out for you

Sweet, to the spirit, soothing and caressing your inner;

Sweet to the psyche, encouraging and supportive;

Sweet to the ear, words warm and pure

Plentiful, a little goes a long way

but you can lay it on thick

Salve for the soul, carrying the antidote to the

chaotic matrix of the societal world, taking you into

a safe sacred space

Shining and glowing, glistening and listening- to

herself, her intuition, the God within

An addition, a multiplier, that takes anything paired

with her to the next level

Drizzle it on, dive in and take it alone, no matter the

portion or method she is an experience and

enhancement

Sweet

Honey

Woman

Won't you wrap me in your love

I wonder, what tombs

are laid

inside your honeycombs

How have you come to embody such an abundance?

Sweet

Honey

Woman